Sheep

Colin Baxter Photography, Grantown-on-Spey, Scotland

Sheep

From the outermost isles to the heart of the lowlands, sheep have shaped the look of many parts of Britain. They have been the moulders of grassy downs, of flower-rich meadows and treeless moors for perhaps 6,000 years, since Neolithic people first brought their livestock and crops to this land.

Now there are more than 60 pure breeds of sheep that have been developed in Britain. That could be one breed for each century of British shepherding and is more than any other country. The range of sizes, shapes and wool colours within that national flock is huge. The smallest, such as the diminutive Shetland, are often richly toned in browns, creams and shades of charcoal and weigh-in at less than 50 kilos. At the other extreme are breeds such as the white-coated Lincoln Longwool, wearer of the heaviest, glossiest fleece in the world, whose rams can be 150 kilos.

Some breeds can be numbered in millions, particularly those in the typical large flocks that graze the uplands. Here, pure-bred natives such as the various kinds of Blackface, the Swaledale and Welsh Mountain are common, with hill sheep such as Cheviot and Beulah on mid-level pastures. Most abundant sheep of all in Britain are 'mules', produced by the mating of older hill ewes to Longwool rams. In the north of England and in Scotland, more than four million such crosses between Blackface or Swaledale ewes and Leicester Longwool rams roam the hills. In Wales, 'Welsh Mules', produced by the mating of ewes from hill breeds such as the Welsh Mountain with Bluefaced Leicester rams, run at more than half-a-million animals.

The Welsh Mule is a fairly recent addition to the British sheep scene, developed in the 1970s to meet demand for fast-growing hill lambs with lean, high quality meat. At the same time, the first imports of Texel sheep from France and the Netherlands were starting to make an impact in the fertile lowlands. Over a handful of decades, the Texel has become one of the most numerous lowland breeds in Britain, while other recent imports, such as the Vendéen and the Bleu du Maine, have also added variety to the national flock.

Much more ancient are some of the island breeds, including the oddly named Manx Loaghtan (from the Isle of Man), the North Ronaldsay (from Orkney), the Hebridean and – oldest of all – the Soay. Present for thousands of years on the remote islands of the St Kilda group, 160 km west of the Scottish mainland, the Soay is one of the most primitive 'domestic' sheep breeds in the world. Like many such primitive sheep, it scatters, rather than bunches, when approached by a dog. This makes it tricky to herd, since the use of trained sheepdogs can be a mainstay of shepherding work with more recent breeds.

Nowadays, the national flock holds some 19 million breeding sheep, tended by around 60,000 shepherds. The bulk of these animals are ewes, with a much smaller number of rams. In the late 1990s, for example, 471,000 rams serviced the mating needs of more than 18 million ewes. That's a ewe-to-ram ratio of 38-to-one. It reflects a typical pattern in hoofed grazing animals, where males try to breed with a large number of females, and play no part, other than flock defence, in rearing of the young, leaving the females sole responsibility for their offspring. For a ewe, this can often mean raising twins and sometimes triplets.

Travel the length of Britain, from the North Isles to the south coast and beyond, and you can still see regional variations in the flocks, from the small sheep of some islands, to the hardy Blackfaces of the hills, the large, meaty sheep of the lowlands and the chunky, curly-fleeced sheep of the South Downs. It's a pattern that reflects millennia of careful selection of sheep qualities that match particular local areas. So in one sense, it's a sign of human enterprise and the sheer adaptability of sheep.

At another, quite simply, it can be beautiful – as much a part of regional contrasts as the shifts from mountains to river valleys, heaths to green pastures. And when the lambs are out and gambolling in spring, sheep – wherever they are – add a touch of something special to the scene.

More than any other domesticated creature, the sheep has helped people to live in remote parts of the British uplands where soils are poor and the weather harsh. The technology of shepherding may change, but the principles have been the same for generations. Wool is easy to transport, slow to rot and has many uses, from clothing to carpets. It has been the gold of many hills and dales in the past, lamb and mutton the silver.

Different breeds of pure-bred sheep are closely linked to different parts of Britain. One of the most characterful is the Herdwick (right). The Herdwick's heartland is the central and western parts of the Lake District, where flocks roam the very highest of fells. Its name comes from the old word 'Herdwyck', which means 'sheep pasture'. With a tough, thick fleece, a Herdwick is one of the hardiest of hill breeds. Its fleece is useful for making carpets.

Few other creatures symbolise spring so well as young lambs. Whatever the breed, they seem to be born cute. Ewes are very attentive, and lick their newborns dry before offering them a drink of warm milk. This first milk, called 'colostrum', holds vital antibodies that help to protect lambs from infection.

It takes about five months of pregnancy for a ewe to produce a lamb. So if spring lambs are part of the plan on a farm, late autumn and early winter will be the period when rams and ewes are let loose together. So that the farmer can tell which ewes have mated, rams can be fitted with boxes of dye on their chests. This makes a coloured mark on a ewe's fleece when the ram mounts her.

Scotland became world-famous for a very different type of breeding in 1997 when the birth of 'Dolly the Sheep' was announced by scientists at the Roslin Institute. The first animal ever to have been cloned from an adult cell (from a mammary gland of a Finn Dorset ewe grown in the womb of a Scottish Blackface). She later produced her own lambs in traditional fashion.

In sunny weather, life can be simple for a ewe and lamb, such as this dapper duo of Blackfaces on the Isle of Lewis (left). But the reality for lamb, ewe and shepherd can be much tougher. Births at night in snowstorms can be part of the picture. Bring on the blizzards, and a good fleece can be a lifesaver. Of all the world's fleeces, few are as famous for their combination of warmth and lightness as that of the Merino, displayed to good effect here by a Merino ewe and lamb (bottom right). Wool like this could eventually be used to make base-layers for people such as mountain bikers and ramblers to wear. For sheep braving the winter elements, food in the form of rows of turnips and shelter from a windbreak of trees can help them to cope. And a nuzzle from mum can also be nice.

Sheep have two teats, so twins are fine for a ewe. Triplets are trickier for both mother and shepherd, meaning that one or more lambs might need to be fostered with another ewe, or bottle-fed. Sheep's milk is rich in minerals and fat: ideal for supporting the rapid growth of lambs until weaning (often at 8-9 weeks old).

Sheep have strong skulls, with those of rams particularly reinforced to cope with clashes during the mating season. Ewes make up the bulk of most flocks, and many will be related to each other. The whole flock, lambs included, benefits from the knowledge of the terrain held by the woolly sisterhood.

Long-woolled, short-fleeced, rare or common, sheep add character and colour to the British rural scene.

British sheep produce around 37 million kilos of wool every year, with some breeds, such as Longwools, yielding fleeces as heavy as 10 kilos apiece. That's an amazing amount of renewable resource, since a single sheep can provide several good fleeces in its lifetime. Changing those fleeces into finished products as varied as knitwear, carpets, tweed jackets and house insulation involves many different processes and a host of skilled workers at each stage. The wool from different breeds can be suited to very different purposes. A Shetland sheep's fleece, for example, might eventually make lace or a Fair Isle jumper, while a North of England Mule's might make help to make a good carpet.

It takes a year for a sheep to grow a full fleece. Primitive breeds, such as the Soay, shed their wool naturally to help them keep cool in summer. But for most of the breeds that have been developed by people, removal of the old fleece by shearing is an essential part of their welfare. A skilled shearer can part a sheep from its fleece, with no harm to the animal, in between two and three minutes.

Sheep grazing favours some plants, especially grasses, and reduces others, such as trees and shrubs. With careful attention to the number of animals used and when they are allowed to graze particular pastures, farmers can produce beautiful, wildlife-rich greenswards with their flocks. The flowery downlands of southern England and the meadows of the Pennines benefit from such careful grazing. So too do the 'machair' grasslands along the Atlantic fringe of the Hebrides.

From hillsides to seashores, heaths to river meadows, sheep have been part of the British rural scene since Neolithic times. Over 60 breeds have developed here. They add to the distinctiveness of our regions and support many jobs, from upland shepherds to city-based carpet makers.

First published in Great Britain in 2008 by
Colin Baxter Photography Ltd
Grantown-on-Spey
PH26 3NA, Scotland

www.colinbaxter.co.uk

Text by Kenny Taylor © Colin Baxter Photography Ltd. 2008
Photographs © 2008 by: Ardea/Duncan Usher: page 15.   Ardea/John Daniels: page 9.
Colin Baxter: pages 5, 10, 13 (top left), 13 (top right), back cover.   Lee Beel: page 8 (left).
britainonview/Alan Novelli: page 14.   Mark Boulton: page 1.   Serena Bowles: page 11.
Laurie Campbell: front cover, pages 8 (bottom right), 12, 17.   Mark Hamblin: page 23.

Mark Hicken: pages 16, 23.   Tony Howell: page 18 (top right).
Wayne Hutchinson/Farm Images: pages 7, 18 (bottom left), 18 (bottom right), 24.
Paul Mayall: page 2.   Neil McIntyre: page 13 (bottom left).   Thomas Mueller: pages 13
(bottom right), 19.   Rafael Ostgathe: page 20.   John Rosenberg: page 21.
Glyn Satterley: pages 6, 18 (top left).   Ann & Steve Toon: page 8 (top right).

ISBN 978-1-84107-398-9   Printed in China